Soul on Fire

Vivekan Jeyagaran

BookLeaf
Publishing

Presentation by *BookLeaf Publishing*

Web: www.bookleafpub.com

E-mail: info@bookleafpub.com

ISBN: 9789357612241

First edition 2022

DEDICATION

I'd like to dedicate this collection to those in the world who have lived through injustice, inequality, and oppression and continue to fight to build a better world for all who share it. Your lived experiences, resistance, and resilience does not go unnoticed. This includes the planet itself, the one that has nurtured us unconditionally for many centuries.

ACKNOWLEDGEMENT

I'd like to acknowledge the warm hearted, wise, and resilient people of Malawi, Laos, my own Tamil community, and many others in Canada and outside whose inspiration has gradually accumulated into this collection. Along the way, many friends have shared their interpretations of these works and their words of encouragement that have fueled the purpose of this collection. A select few have encouraged me to bring these ideas to life on these pages, as they themselves led by example and reminded me that these words do indeed have a place in the world; you know who you are.

There is then my family, who have always been the anchors. They have been a group of people who have always had a deep appreciation for creative expression, storytelling, and soulful encounters. Their understanding, respect, and appreciation for all forms of art through their own exploration of poetry, visual arts, and music, were the seeds that were planted early on.

Zikomo, Khop Chai, Thank You, and Nandri.

A Forgotten Justice

When leaves fall, trees may refuse to die,
Upon rainfall, the clouds may still be alive in the sky.
When life bearing roots, are crushed however,
Even the greatest of Palmyra's, shall certainly
whither.

Amidst the screams, of a roaring sea,
Through the rolling hills, of agonizing tea,
Comes a desperate cry, seeking a forgotten justice,
Yet drowned away, by selective blindness.

Isolated in solitude, from the rest of the world,
Floating all alone, having once been impearled,
A lonely teardrop, the pearl of the Indian Ocean,
Awaiting the jury, to revoke its absurd absolution.

There stands a Palmyra, on rocky foundation,
As the remainder are chained, with no concession.
There stand a people, plagued by corruption,
As we wait desperately, for that deserving resolution.

When the sun rests, the flowers continue to bloom,
After our lives end, souls live on in new costume,
When the ocean shatters, into ripples however,
Even the most spiritual of lands, may certainly
shiver.

Lest We Forget

Look into your mirrors, for it's been a while,
Having crossed the seas, for freedom in exile.
Recall the blood red soil, that houses our ancestry,
For we must not surrender, our island's history.

Observe the way, history crafts our stories,
Painting a portrait, of us on our knees.
Weaving fact and fiction, into a single narrative,
Stories so seductive, they hold us all captive.

National stories, muddled with hypocrisy,
Claiming the entitlement, bred from ancestry.
One that is as tainted, as pure supremacy,
Leading this pearl, into moral bankruptcy.

Single narratives, that capture our stories,
Layers of our history, thrown to the breeze.
Enslaving the truth, and releasing the fear,
Threats to the hegemony, is all that they hear.

Lest we forget, the harvesters of the seas,
Is there an opportunity, that we must seize?
History speaks little, of our people's plight,
But the story ahead, is partially ours to write.

No Shame

Have you no shame little one,
Tormenting any along your path.
Poking both the young and old,
Being the tiniest, yet so bold.

Originating from, who knows where,
You reach new countries through the air,
Yet strip us from all our comforts,
By arresting us in our own homes.

Tiny as you are, deadly is your strength,
Mother Nature's weapon you are.
Punishing the ego of humankind,
We have learned our lessons, no longer blind.

Forgive us for all our sins,
We have exhausted all our options.
Forgive us for our selfish actions,
Show mercy on us shameless humans!

-Guest contribution from Thevaki Jeyagaran
A true poet and admirer of Tamil literature who has paved
the way for this collection and my exploration of poetry

For We Have Forgotten

The rage, the grace, and the ferocity in between,
This relationship promised, to be nothing but pristine.
Yet we stand here confused, as her wrath unravels,
For we have forgotten, our countless betrayals.

We are locked up desperately, living on in fear,
While the once disappearing skies, begin to clear.
Disenfranchised from the mother, paying a karmic
penance,
For we have forgotten, her abundant presence.

Where we once shared a home, in delicate harmony,
Remains a world descending, into natural anarchy.
Now our earthly cohabitants, traverse the silver
lining,
For we have forgotten, this too is their dwelling.

All we were asked of, was a meager compliance,
Yet for far too long, we have lived in ignorance.
We must now pursue, the grandest of amnesty,
For we have forgotten the teachings, of a rich
ancestry.

Kindred Spirits

The rage, the grace, and the ferocity in between,
This relationship promised, to be nothing but
pristine.
Calling out to me desperately, yearning to meet,
Now this is a bond, to which I could always
retreat.

There it goes navigating, through the
undergrowth,
Creating dense and lush bonds, tied by an eternal
oath.
A river giving life, to everything in its path,
This is a land that is borne, from a volcanic
wrath.

The river features no end, nor any beginning,
Forever uninhibited, by the canopy's breathing.
The intimacy deserved, an adventurous tribute,
Enamored by kindred spirits, I follow on in
pursuit.

Fungal networks beneath, never cease to inspire,
Exchanging origin stories, that set the soul on
fire.
Sharing a nurturing love, unconditional and
boundless,
Their grand contributions, remain truly timeless.

As they tower above, serving as watchful
guardian,
Protecting their visitors, cultivating their
attraction.
As a symbiosis is born, that manifests in kinship,
The forest quietly pleads, for our sincere
stewardship.

The harmony, the solace, and the love in
between,
This companionship promised, to be nothing but
pristine.
Calling out to me desperately, yearning to meet,
Now this is a bond, to which I could always
retreat.

- A letter to the natural world

A New Bond

The rolling hills of coffee, and all the life in between,
This relationship promised, to be nothing but pristine,
Calling out to me desperately, yearning to meet,
Now this is a bond, to which I could always retreat.

There it goes navigating, through the undergrowth,
Creating dense and lush bonds, tied by an eternal
oath,
A river giving life, to everything in its path,
This is a land that lives, beyond democracy's
aftermath.

The stream takes me, to the truth of civilization,
Technology absent, amidst an intimate connection.
The blood red soil, furnishing the steady stilt houses,
Where humanity comes to life, in many disguises.

Ambition stronger, than a finely brewed espresso,
A life seeped in tradition, transcends the status-quo,
Manifesting in the coffee, that shoulders the
community,
The elements convene here daily, with sincere
loyalty.

- Inspired by my relationship with
the people of the Bolaven Plateau

Nature's Architect

The karst walls wrap around,
In an intimate embrace,
The city that was crowned,
No longer ruled by its grace.

The paddy sits still,
As they all take a gander,
Far above the hill,
Aspiring high with candor.

The clouds all earthbound,
Leaving empty, the airspace,
They do nothing but astound,
As they fade without a trace.

The curtain gracefully falls,
And the stars make an appearance,
While those karst walls,
Stage a subtle disappearance.

The walls care little,
Of the people they protect,
For they own no credential,
Comparable to nature's architect.

*- Written in awe of the karst mountains of Vang Vieng
and Luang Prabang in Northern Laos*

The Great Providers

Our greatest providers, live on in solace,
Their grand contributions, truly timeless.

An unconditional love, unparalleled and
boundless,
Begins to fade, courtesy of incurable illness.

Our greatest providers, the forests of yesteryear,
Serve their purpose, as unconditional volunteer.

They observe in silence, spreading roots with
humility,
Deferring judgement, avoiding all complacency.

Light Between the Trees

Dancing among the shadows,
Of the light between the trees,
Ancient wisdom is carried,
Through the forest breeze.

This wisdom once protected,
Our valiant ancestors,
But now we are guided,
By the fantasies of realtors.

We now embark on adventures,
Seeking that lost wisdom,
Hoping it will be the key,
To our abundant freedom.

Yet it remains hidden,
In the depths of ancient forestry,
Waiting for that day,
We embrace our modesty.

Brown Gold

The gold that flows, through our elaborate veins,
The crop that is known, by many names,
The gift that alleviates, our daytime pains,
The commodity that plays, one too many games.

Our world is nothing, but a bottomless mine,
Just waiting for the plunder, of humankind.
Oh labourers please, wait your spot in line,
Apparently it was not you, that made this find.

You're right to think, the system needs a
redesign,
For your fate and this chain, are forever
intertwined.
They keep you in your corner, as they wine and
dine,
For it is you not them, contained by this chain's
bind.

Posing as a gift, that elevates their daily grind,
The brown gold is no longer, part of your
bloodline.
It was their chains after all, that made this
incredible find,
As it now flows away, from your native skyline.

You continue to hope, for these chains to be redefined,
To be considered human to them, is asinine.
You believe a consumer movement, would be so inclined,
For you forget that chains were made, to always confine.

Lest we forget, those who work the fields,
Finely brewed lattes, coming from your yields.
History speaks ill, of the people's plight,
But the story ahead, is all of ours to write.

Leopold's Forest of Green

We consume with no deliberation,
While many consume with only hesitation.
We create with little to no oversight,
While others create under Big Brother's
powerful might.

Trees as mighty, as the Empire State,
Stand idle as they give life to a perpetual fate.
Trees as tall, as the one true Everest,
Stand idle as they're caged, under arrest.

The trees give life, to many a golden bean,
So King Leopold can mint, his own forest of
green.
Unconditional love, clearly does not exist,
As kids camp under trees, as their struggles
persist.

The white-collar margins, dwarf even the Burj of
trees,
While those kids' margins, barely keep them off
their knees.
Innovation brings riches, to those endowed with
blonde hair,
While on the roadside, brings only smiles of
despair.

We consume, to climb the social ladder,
While many consume, only things that matter.
We create to satisfy, our financial thirst,
While others create, to settle their hunger first.

Trees as tall as the one Kilimanjaro,
Create the cycle of poverty, that continues
tomorrow.

*- Sparked by encounters with young innovators
using rubber to create and sell homemade
soccer balls in Malawi*

Curse of Abundance

Where is the history, we lost to convenience,
Where is the tradition, we lost to ignorance.
We gave up our ancestry, for everyday access,
We sold our heritage, for everyday low prices.

We once navigated the seas, in search of our
harvest,
Embracing our provider, our catch often modest.
We now navigate the aisles, with a holy
reverence,
Marveling at the choices, admiring corporate
abundance.

Where red chillies once bathed, in tropical sun
rays,
Plastic containers stand idle, transcending expiry
days.
Where the paddy once stood still, dancing to the
breeze,
Ready-made biryani, sits with frozen peas.

Our lands were once gifted, with natural
abundance,
Now our lives are cursed, with time and
convenience.
And the Palmyra lies flat, lamenting our
absence,
As ancestors of yesteryear, register their
grievance.

Where is the tradition, we lost to convenience,
Where is the art, we lost to ignorance.
We gave up our ancestry, for everyday access,
We sold our mastery, for everyday low prices.

We often taken more, than we happen to leave,
So honour your planet, every Christmas Eve.
Consumption cares little, of our planet's plight,
But the story ahead, is ours to write.

Deal with the Devil

There they were, in our time of need,
Providing and sharing, our daily feed.
Persuaded by, everyday low prices,
We simply had to, ignore their disguises.

Little did we know, a deal with the devil,
Formed the foundation, of our fragile castle.
Relishing in, the profit of our ignorance,
They now ignore, all forms of defiance.

An Enslaved Truth

We envy the way, you craft our stories,
Painting a portrait, of those who cross the seas,
Weaving fact and fiction, into a single narrative,
Stories so seductive, you hold us all captive.

We are fascinated by, your elite hypocrisy,
Claiming the entitlement, bred from your ancestry.
One that is as tainted, as your pure supremacy,
Leading the world, into moral bankruptcy.

We envy the way, you capture our stories,
The layers of our existence, thrown to the breeze,
While enslaving the truth, and releasing the fear,
You claim your rights, whilst endowed in our
cashmere.

We are fascinated by, your elite mongering,
Pushing a narrative, that borders on enlightening,
While effortlessly ignoring, the shades of our life,
While leaving our world, with unimaginable strife.

Taking Refuge

The pollen of flowers,
Are taken with no choice,
Travelling across many acres,
They find refuge, without rejoice.

They feed the circle of life,
Fuelling the perpetual cycle,
Continuing with little to no strife,
Comes a system, now ancestral.

Do they desire to return,
To reclaim what was taken?
Is it not this for what they yearn,
Or is this refuge, their best bargain?

They were pried with no agency,
Tasked with greasing the wheel.
Now this system has become an ancestry,
But a day will come, for the great reveal.

Our Future to Write

Cherishing the right, to live as we please,
Throwing obligation away, into the breeze,
Guided by illusion, our aspirational fantasy,
Pursuing false truths, a life void of entropy.

The scars accumulate, into a moral stockpile,
Leading us to inevitable, freedom in exile.
We stand here today, ignoring our moral
obligation,
We have yet to earn, an official absolution.

Lest we forget, those who crossed the seas,
Is this not an opportunity, that we must seize?
History speaks ill, of our people's plight,
But the story ahead, is ours to write.

You Are

You are not the colour of your skin,
Nor thy family name,
You are not your ancestors,
Nor the riches that come with fame,
You are not your profession,
Nor the product of the imperial game.

You are the product of those before,
And the legacy of those who follow,
You are the strangers you've met,
And the friends you've lost,
You are the relationships that you beget,
The world's greatest vignette.

You are the place you've been
And the stories you've heard,
You are the things you've seen,
And the memories spurred.

-Inspired by Hemingway's poem of the same
name

Legacy

The wheel is spun, nearing the end of its adventure,
As it presents its gift, and bids farewell forever,
The silkworm managed, to illustrate its mastery,
A gift that was borne, from an ancient tapestry.

The world spins around, and like that we are born,
We countdown the clock, until the day we mourn.
A legacy means little, even to those who achieve,
For we often take more, than we happen to leave.

We consume abundantly, with no deliberation,
While ignorance has become, our one true addiction.
Escape the invisible hand, and the branded textile,
Liberate yourself, and find freedom in exile.

Ignore the cynical voice, that comes in many
disguises,
Charading as realism, conspiring so your dream
collapses.
You are not being judged, by anyone that matters,
So stop trying to race, up these fabricated ladders.

The wheel is spun, and the silk is twirled,
As it presents its gift, and perishes from the world,
The silkworm managed, to create a legacy,
A gift that was borne, by mandate of destiny.

Only Words

You grant us, permission to wander,
You beget, new quests to ponder.

You transport us, to whole new worlds,
You illustrate, using only words.

You spark, philosophical revolution,
You revoke, political resignation.

You trap us, in a cycle of curiosity,
You transform us, with unmatched velocity.

You are the stories of yesteryear's minds.
You are the wisdom hiding in these binds.

You are the legacy of those before,
And inspiring the stories of those that follow.